LEARN TO PLAY
MORE EASY PIANO CLASSICS

Caroline Phipps

Designed by Lindy Dark
Illustrated by Peter Dennis

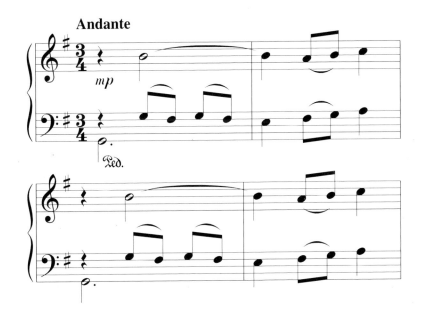

Music arrangements by Caroline Phipps
Music engravings by Michael Durnin

Series editor: Anthony Marks

With thanks to Emma Danes

Contents

Introduction

The tunes in this book are all taken from famous pieces of classical music. Some of the pieces were originally written for the piano, but others were written for an orchestra, or a group of instruments or singers. They have been specially arranged and simplified to make them easy to play. Many of them should be familiar, even those with titles that you may not recognize.

The pieces are grouped in four sections. At the beginning of each one there is an introduction to the music that follows. Near the end of the book, there are some hints about how to play each piece.

Naming and numbering pieces of music

Most pieces of music have a number, called an opus number. (Opus is the Latin word for "work"). In this book, opus numbers have been used when the composer wrote more than one piece with the same title. Where a piece has a well-known title, no opus number has been given.

Sometimes a single opus number was given to a group of pieces that were published together. In this case each piece was given a second number, for example, op.35, no.5. The opus number will help you if you want to buy a recording of a particular piece, or a copy of the original music for it.

Theatre music

Since the earliest times, music has been a very important part of theatrical performances. Music is often added to plays to make them more interesting. Sometimes musicians accompany singing and dancing on stage, but music can also be used to emphasize the mood of the play, rather like film or television music.

Inside an opera house

Acting, singing and dancing have always been closely linked. In ancient Greek and Roman times, some actors used to mime the story (act without speaking) while music was played. Later, composers began to write music to go with plays and religious stories. Gradually, two special kinds of theatre music developed. One, opera, is based on singing. The other, ballet, is based on dancing.

Opera

Opera tells a story through songs. The music is played by an orchestra, while the actors sing on stage. The first opera was performed in the early 17th century.

La Scala opera house in Milan

Opera soon became very popular in Europe, and many opera houses (special theatres for opera) were built.

Opening of *Orfeo*, an early opera

The performers were often much more famous than the composers. People would go to an opera to hear singers they liked.

Title page of an opera by Mozart

There are lots of different types of opera. The styles have changed gradually over the years. In Handel's operas, all the words are sung, and the stories are serious. They are often based on history or mythology. Several of Mozart's operas, including *The Marriage of Figaro* and *Così fan tutte*, are based on comical stories and contain spoken parts. In the 19th century, composers like Verdi and Puccini wrote operas with sad, romantic stories. These are often about the lives of ordinary people, not historical or legendary ones.

The story used in an opera is called the libretto. This is the Italian word for 'little book'. When opera first began, the people in the audience had this in front of them so that they could read the words while the opera was being performed. Later, the audience sat in the dark, and only the stage was lit. This made it too dark to read, but it was easier to see what was happening on the stage.

Title page of Verdi's *La traviata*

Ballet

Ballet tells a story using music and dance. There are no spoken words, so the music is very descriptive and the dancers use their movements to tell the story.

The first ballets were performed in private. Wealthy noblemen arranged evenings of entertainment in their homes, in which performers sang, danced and recited poetry.

Modern ballet dancers

Performers at a private house

The dances gradually became the most important part, and the performers started to mime the actions instead of singing or reciting words. The first ballet to be shown in a public theatre was staged in 1581 in France.

At first, dancers chose any music to perform to. It was not necessarily dance music.

Later, composers such as Lully began to write music specially for the ballet. Someone else worked out the dance steps. The person who arranges the dances is called the choreographer.

Ballet stories are very imaginative. Some are based on fairy tales, like the ballets of Delibes and Tchaikovsky. Two of the most popular ballets in this style are Tchaikovsky's *The Nutcracker* and *The Sleeping Beauty*. Other ballets are based on plays or books, and can be sad or romantic.

Overtures

An overture is a piece of music that is played before an opera or ballet begins. It is the first music that the audience hears, so it is often lively and exciting to attract people's attention.

Overtures are also played at the beginning of orchestral concerts. The overture to Rossini's opera *The Barber of Seville* is often used this way. When this idea first became popular, many composers, such as Mendelssohn, began writing overtures specially for concerts.

A scene in *The Nutcracker*

Costumes and scenery

Opera and ballet often use spectacular costumes and scenery. Sometimes parts of the scenery have to move during the performance.

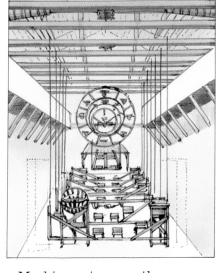

17th century opera scenery

Often complex machinery is needed to do this. This can make ballets and operas very expensive to stage.

Machinery to move the scenery shown above

Terzettino

This tune is from a light-hearted opera called *Così fan tutte* by Wolfgang Amadeus Mozart (1756-1791). It was written in 1790.

Terzettino means "a little trio". It is a song for three people. On the left is a page of music from the opera in Mozart's handwriting.

Mozart

On the right is a scene from a performance of *Così fan tutte*. It took place in 1969 at a festival in Salzburg, the city where Mozart was born.

The words of the opera (the libretto) were written by Lorenzo da Ponte. He also wrote the words for two of Mozart's other operas.

Fidelio

Ludwig van Beethoven (1770-1827) wrote many kinds of music. But although he was interested in theatre music, *Fidelio* was his only opera.

At first, audiences disliked the opera. Beethoven rewrote it several times before it was a success. On the left you can see a scene from the opera.

Beethoven

The Barber of Seville overture

Gioachino Rossini (1792-1868) was a very famous and successful composer. He wrote *The Barber of Seville* in 1816 for a theatre in Rome.

It was performed less than a month after he started to write it. Many people think it is one of the best comic operas ever written.

Rossini

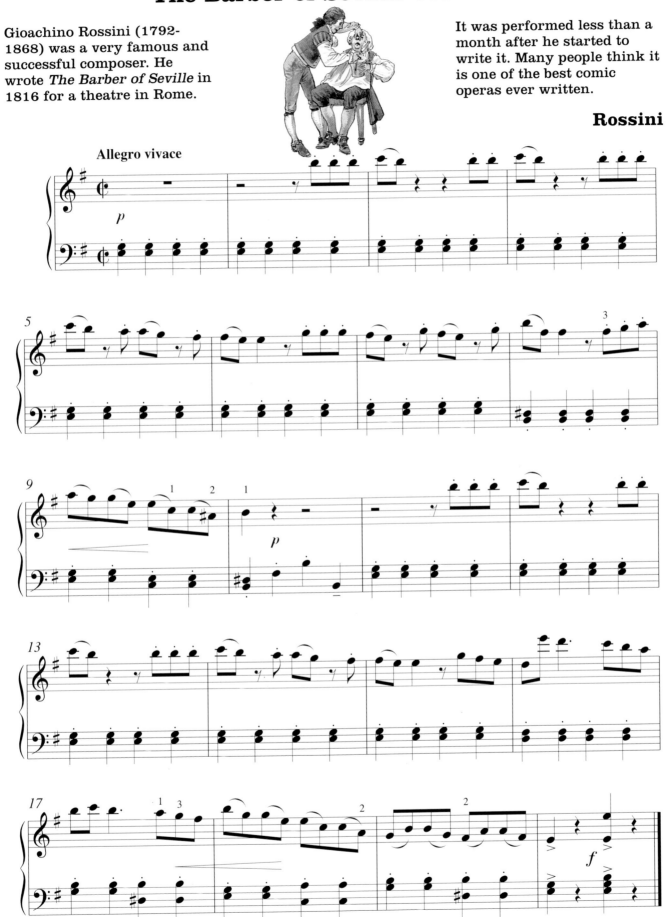

Drinking song

This tune is from an opera by Giuseppe Verdi (1813-1901) called *La traviata*. It is now one of the most popular operas ever written.

But the first performance in 1853 was not a success. This is partly because it used modern costumes like the one on the left.

Verdi

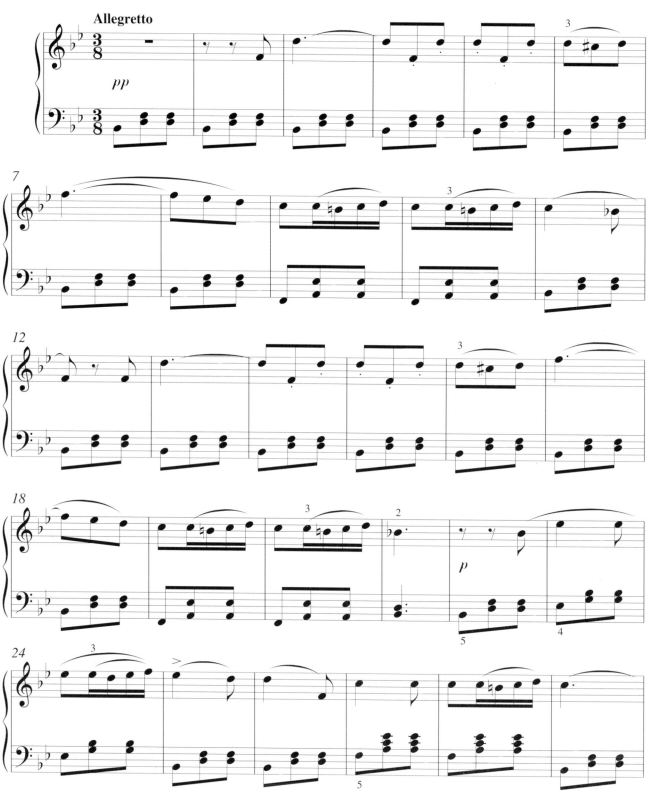

This made the sad story too
realistic. At the time, people
thought that operas should
be like fantasies, and not like
real life.

In some later performances,
the singers had 17th-century
costumes like the one shown
here. This helped the opera
become much more popular.

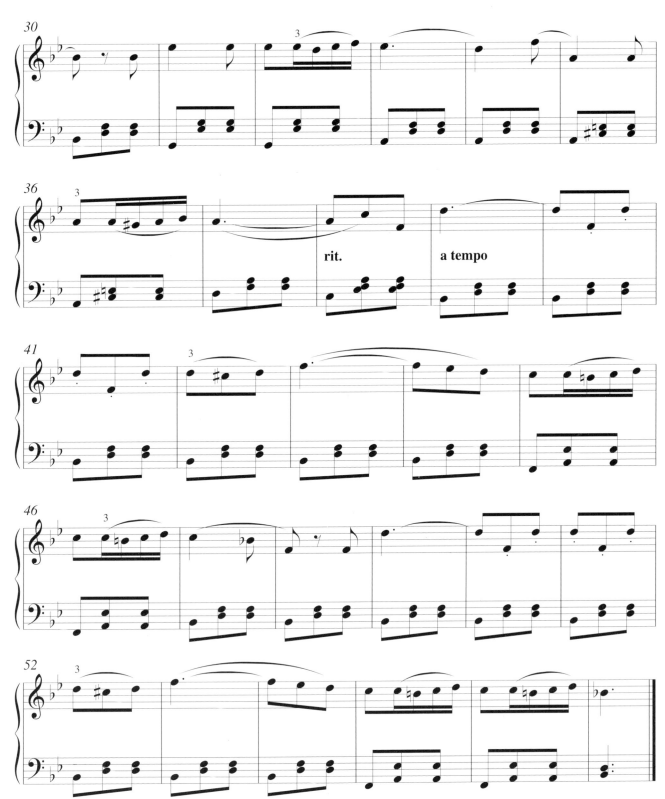

Anvil chorus

This song is from another opera by Verdi called *Il trovatore* which means "The troubadour". A troubadour was a medieval poet.

It was written at the same time as *La traviata* (see page 10). Verdi finished the two operas within six weeks of each other.

Verdi

The story of *Il trovatore*

The Count di Luna and the troubadour Manrico are brothers, but they do not know this. The Count believes his brother was killed by a woman called Azucena, but in fact she has brought up Manrico as her own child. The Count sentences Azucena to death for murdering his brother. When Manrico tries to save her, the Count imprisons him.

The two men are in love with the same woman, Leonore, though she loves Manrico. To save him, she agrees to marry the count. But at the last minute she poisons herself, and Manrico is killed. Only then does the Count discover that Manrico was his brother.

Manrico serenades Leonore with love songs

12

The *Anvil chorus* is sung by people beating metal on an anvil. The bass line of the music imitates the crash of the hammer.

On the left is some scenery used in a performance of the opera. The troubadour comes to this castle to sing to Leonore, the woman he loves.

Manrico and the Count fight a duel over Leonore

Leonore and Manrico are happy until the Count arrests Manrico

Leonore begs the Count to spare Manrico's life

Soldiers' chorus

This tune is from an opera called *Faust* by Charles Gounod (1818-1893). It is based on a story by the German writer Goethe.

In the story, Faust sells his soul to the Devil. Several other composers, including Mendelssohn and Berlioz, also wrote music based on it.

Gounod

14

March of the kings

This piece is by Georges Bizet (1838-1875), shown on the right. It was written for *L'Arlésienne*, a play by the French writer Daudet.

The tune itself is a very old folk song. It comes from Provence, the area in the south of France where Daudet lived.

Bizet

Du und du

This tune is by Johann Strauss II (1825-1899). It is from an operetta (short, light-hearted opera) called *Die Fledermaus* ("The bat").

Strauss wrote 16 other operettas. On the left you can see a picture from the title page of *Die Fledermaus* showing Strauss as a bat.

Strauss

Morning

This tune is by Edvard Grieg (1843-1907). It is part of some music he was asked to write by Henrik Ibsen, a Norwegian author.

The music was written to go with Ibsen's play *Peer Gynt*. This part describes Peer Gynt waking up and seeing the sun rising in the desert.

Grieg

Flower duet

This tune is from an opera called *Lakmé* by Léo Delibes (1836-1891). It was successful immediately because of its oriental style.

At this time oriental fashions were very popular. They influenced music, painting, poetry and even the style of dress some people wore.

Delibes

Delibes was very interested in theatre music. He was chorus master at the Opéra in Paris. On the right you can see the singer Lily Pons as Lakmé.

The sign ℘ed. under a note tells you to press the pedal on the right, and to hold it down for the full length of the note.

Pizzicati

This tune is from a ballet called *Sylvia*. It is one of Delibes' most famous pieces, along with another of his ballets, *Coppélia*.

The title means "plucked". In this piece the string players have to pluck their instruments, not bow them. This makes a special sound.

Delibes

Sleeping Beauty waltz

This tune is from a ballet by Pyotr Il'yich Tchaikovsky (1840-1893), based on a fairy tale. It was written in 1890 in St. Petersburg.

The picture shows the prince discovering Sleeping Beauty. He kisses her and wakes her up, breaking the spell of the wicked witch.

Tchaikovsky

Music for dancing

Dancing has always been a popular entertainment. At first, most people danced privately in their homes, or at feasts and parties. But, in the 18th and 19th centuries, as more people wanted to dance, large public halls called ballrooms were opened. An orchestra or small band played the music. There were many types of dance. Each one changed little by little over many years, but some of them are still danced today.

Music for dancing is different from music for ballet (see page 5). Ballet music was written for professional dancers and theatrical performances, but most of the music in this section of the book was written for ordinary people to dance to.

An 18th century ballroom

Early dances

In ancient times, dances were used as a way of praying. People danced and sang to ask their gods to make crops grow. But this died out in most parts of Europe when Christianity became the most common religion. We know from books and pictures that dancing was still popular, but very little dance music from before about 1350 has been found. This is probably because the only music written down in this period was church music (see page 36). But gradually people began to write folk and dance music down too.

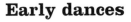

Medieval dancers

Early folk music

16th century dancers

During the 15th and 16th centuries, the basse danse was very popular. This was in fact a series of dances in several different styles. However the music was never very fast because the clothes people wore were so bulky that they were not able to move quickly.

The suite

By the Baroque period (about 1600 to 1750) the basse danse had developed into a musical form called the suite. This is a set of dances played one after the other.

There was no limit to the number of dances, but normally there were four or five. The most popular dances were the allemande, the courante, the sarabande and the gigue. Any extra ones were inserted between the sarabande and the gigue.

In the allemande the dancers linked arms. It was a good dance to begin with because it was not too fast. The courante used quick running steps. Sometimes it was hard for the dancers to keep up with the music.

18th century dancers

After this, the slow, gentle sarabande gave the dancers a rest. The suite usually ended with a fast, lively gigue.

The minuet

The minuet was another dance which was often included in the suite. Minuets are slow and graceful, in three-four or three-eight time. The dancing couples bow to each other and point their toes as they dance.

In the 18th century, the minuet was one of the most popular dances. Even when it was no longer fashionable in ballrooms, composers continued to write minuets to include in their operas, ballets and symphonies.

One of the most famous composers of waltzes was Johann Strauss II, the son of another composer called Johann Strauss.

Title page of *The Blue Danube*

The gavotte and musette

The gavotte became popular around the end of the Baroque period. It was often included in suites.

Another dance, called the musette, developed from the gavotte. It is similar in style, but the bass line contains a repeated note known as a drone. This sometimes makes the music sound a bit like a bagpipe. At around this time in France, a small bagpipe called a musette was very popular.

Dancing a minuet

Mozart wrote lots of minuets. Some were for dancing, but others were part of larger pieces of music like operas and ballets.

The 19th century

The most popular dance in the 19th century was the waltz. It is in three-four time, and is quite fast. Some people believed the waltz was unhealthy because the dancing couples whirled around the room so quickly.

Another very popular dance in the 19th century was the polonaise. This originally came from Poland in the 16th century. The polonaise was slow and dignified, and was often danced at weddings and other special occasions.

In the 19th century, many composers began to feel very proud of the customs and traditions of their countries. They began writing music that was based on folk tunes and dances. This is known as Nationalism. Famous nationalist pieces are Grieg's Norwegian dances and Dvořák's Slavonic dances.

A musette

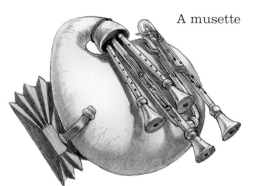

One of the most famous musettes was written by Johann Sebastian Bach, in his *Notebook for Anna Magdalena Bach*.

19th century dancers waltzing

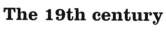

23

Musette

J.S. Bach (1685-1750) came from a very musical family. His father was a musician and three of his sons became famous composers.

This piece is from a book of music he wrote for his wife, Anna Magdalena. The picture shows him accompanying his family singing and playing.

J. S. Bach

German dance

The German dance had three beats to the bar and people danced it in pairs. The two main kinds were the ländler and the waltz.

The ländler involved hopping and stamping. The waltz was more elegant. Haydn, Beethoven and Schubert also wrote German dances.

Mozart

Minuet in A

Luigi Boccherini (1743-1805) wrote this minuet as one movement of a string quintet (a piece of music for five stringed instruments).

Music for small groups of instruments is often called chamber music. It became very popular around this time.

Boccherini

Moderato

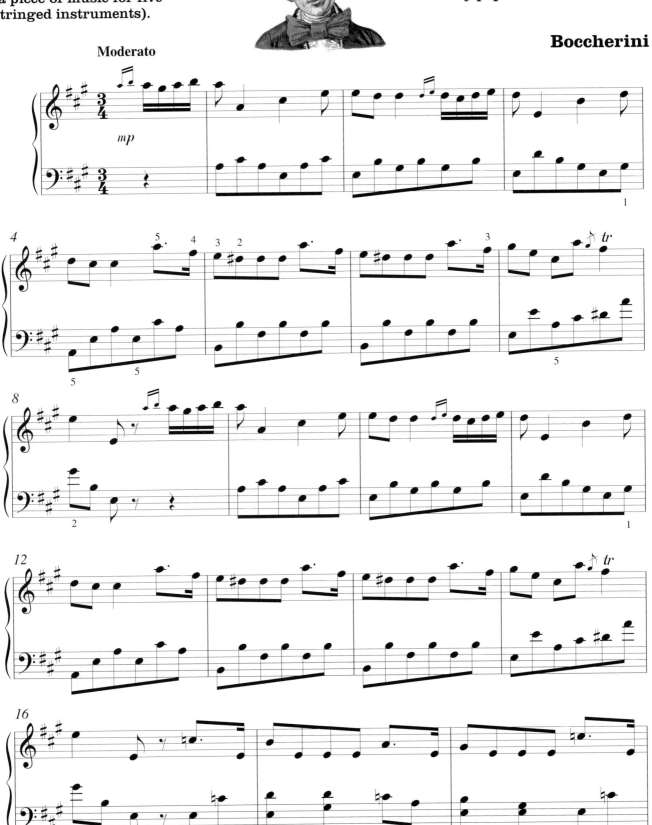

Boccherini wrote over 120 string quintets and about 90 string quartets (for four stringed instruments). He was also a talented cellist.

Like many other composers at this time, he usually wrote a minuet as the third movement of his string quartets and quintets.

The Blue Danube waltz no.1

Johann Strauss composed this waltz in 1867. He was asked to write some music to accompany a poem about the Austrian capital city, Vienna.

The poem included the words "Vienna, be glad, Oho, why, why?" Many Viennese people felt insulted by this.

Strauss

Later, when the words had been removed, the tune became extrememly popular. It was almost like an unofficial national anthem.

Strauss' original copy of the opening is shown here. The full title is *An der schönen blauen Donau* ("By the beautiful blue Danube").

Hungarian dance no.5

Johannes Brahms (1833-1897) was born in Hamburg in Germany. He wrote 21 Hungarian dances for piano between 1868 and 1880.

There were many Hungarian people living in Hamburg at this time. Brahms heard a great deal of Hungarian folk music as a child.

Brahms

Dance of the hours

Amilcare Ponchielli (1834-1886) taught at the music school in Milan in Italy. One of his pupils was Puccini, another famous composer.

Dance of the hours is from an opera called *La gioconda* ("The joyful girl") written in 1876. It is Ponchielli's most famous opera.

Ponchielli

Slavonic dance op.46, no.8

Antonin Dvořák (1841-1904) was born in Bohemia, now called the Czech Republic. Many of his pieces were based on Czech folk tunes.

On the left is the title on the cover of his Slavonic dances. It was one of the first pieces he was commissioned to write, and was very popular.

Dvořák

Eugene Onegin waltz

Tchaikovsky wrote this piece in 1879. It was performed in Moscow the same year. It is based on a story by Pushkin, a Russian poet.

On the left is a picture of Tchaikovsky's country house. It was half-way between Moscow and St. Petersburg.

Tchaikovsky

Norwegian dance op.35, no.2

Grieg went to a special music school (shown on the right) called the Leipzig Conservatoire, in Germany.

The school was founded by another composer called Mendelssohn (see page 50) in 1843, the year in which Grieg was born.

Grieg

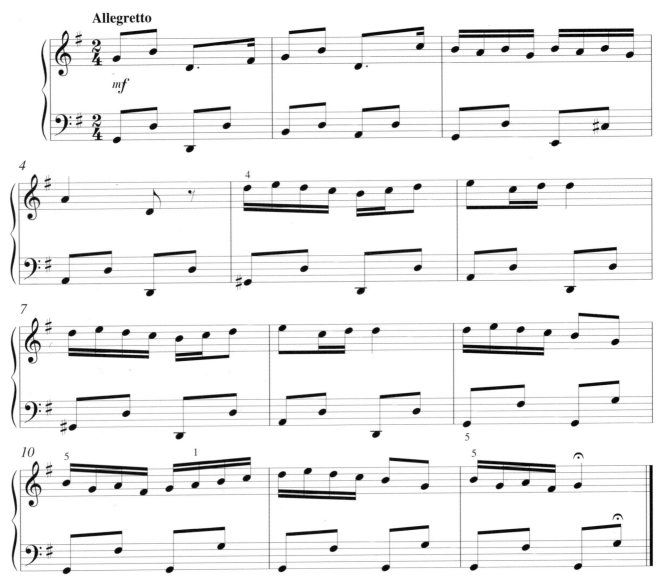

Grieg was very influenced by Norwegian folk music. A lot of his pieces, including this dance, are written in a traditional Norwegian style. Some of his pieces were based on folk stories, or were written to describe the Norwegian landscape. He also wrote many songs using poems by Norwegian writers. Many of these were first performed by his wife, Nina Hagerup, a famous singer. In 1867 Grieg founded the Norwegian Academy of Music, so that other Norwegian composers could learn to write music in a traditional style.

Norwegian folk dancers

34

Polovtsian dance no.1

This dance is from an opera called *Prince Igor*. Alexander Borodin (1833-1887) worked on this opera for 18 years but died before it was finished.

The opera was completed by two other composers, Rimsky-Korsakov and Glazunov. Like Borodin, both of them were Russian.

Borodin

Religious music

People have always used music for prayers to their gods and goddesses, in different religions all over the world. The earliest surviving written music was composed for use in churches. The pieces in this section of the book were written for worship in different types of Christian churches.

St. Mark's Cathedral, Venice

Early church music

The first type of church music is known as plainsong or plainchant. It was first written down in the 6th century AD, but may have been used for many years before that. Each prayer had its own chant, and there were different chants for various times of the year. The tunes were very slow and only used a few notes.

13th century music (left)

16th century music (right)

Beside plainsong, the only other popular music was folk music. Folk songs were lively and tuneful, and so were enjoyable to sing. In the 10th century, some composers began to think that they could make their church music more interesting if

they mixed chants with folk tunes. Gradually church music became more varied.

Early folk musicians

Church composers

Until the 17th century, most composers were paid by churches to write music. In many large churches, the composers had to write new music for every week. This was performed in church by professional musicians, at first an organist and a choir, later an orchestra too.

Later composers did not have to depend on churches for their money. But some still worked for churches, and others wrote church music for special occasions. In the 19th century, some composers wrote religious music that they intended to be played in concert halls, rather than in church.

The mass

A mass is a type of religious service (set of prayers) held in many Christian churches. Masses have special words, usually in Latin, that are spoken by the priest. In the 7th century, composers began to set the words of the mass to music. At first the tunes were chants. Later they became more complicated, and parts for instruments were added.

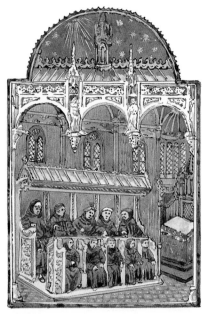

Medieval monks singing mass

For hundreds of years, the mass was the most popular form of church music.

There are masses for many different occasions. As well as ordinary ones for each day of the year, there are masses for special events like coronations, weddings and funerals. A funeral mass is called a requiem ("re-kwi-em"). It gets its name from the Latin words "Requiem in pace" which means "May they rest in peace".

The chorale

In Germany in the 16th century, some church leaders believed that people should take part in prayers, not just listen to the choir or orchestra. One of these, Martin Luther, began writing tunes for everybody to sing. They had words that were written in everyday languages, not Latin. These

An 18th century performance of an oratorio

tunes are called chorales, and they were usually accompanied by an organ.

Some chorale tunes are based on plainchant melodies, others on folk songs. The melodies were simpler than most masses of the time. This made them easier to sing and meant that everyone could join in. J. S. Bach was one of the most important composers of chorales.

Martin Luther

Soon this type of church singing became popular all over northern Europe and later in America. Today, tunes in this style are often called hymns. Some are based on earlier chorales, but there are many recent ones too.

The oratorio

An oratorio is a piece of music that tells a story based on scenes from the Bible. It is sung by a choir and is usually accompanied by a small group of instruments or by an orchestra.

Oratorios were developed by a group of church leaders who were trying to encourage more people to go to church. They believed that people would find stories from the Bible much more interesting if they were presented in this way. Opera was very popular at around this time, so many composers started to develop a musical style similar to opera for writing oratorios.

Sometimes they added hymns and chorales. But oratorios were not intended to be performed on stage, and the singers do not wear costumes or act out the parts. The main parts are sung by soloists and the rest by the choir.

Spirituals

Spirituals are religious songs that developed in America during the 18th and 19th centuries. They are sung in churches in the same way as hymns, but the style of music is often different from hymns.

People singing spirituals

This is because they are more closely related to folk songs. By the end of the 19th century, spiritual songs had become very popular as concert pieces. Because of this, spirituals used in church services began to change, and a new form of religious music developed. This new style became known as gospel music.

Hymn singing in the 19th century

Wachet auf!

Wachet auf! is a cantata (a piece for choir or solo singers with an orchestra). It is usually known in English as "Sleepers wake".

Bach wrote *Wachet auf* in 1731. This tune from it is a chorale (see p.37). It is called "Zion hears!"

J. S. Bach

Bach wrote over 200 church cantatas. This one is number 140. He also wrote a lot of other church music, such as oratorios and masses.

Bach was the director of St. Thomas' Church in Leipzig from 1723 until he died. On the left you can see him directing his church choir.

Jesu, joy of man's desiring

This piece is also from a cantata. It is a very popular tune and many people have tried to write music that sounds similar to it.

On the left you can see the town of Leipzig where Bach lived and worked for most of his life.

J. S. Bach

The Heavens are telling the glory of God

This song is from an oratorio (see page 37) called *The Creation* by Joseph Haydn (1732-1809). It is about the creation of the world.

The picture shows the palace of Esterháza in Hungary. This is where Haydn worked for the princes Paul Anton and Nicholas Esterházy.

Haydn

The Lord's my shepherd

The tune of this hymn was written in the middle of the 19th century by Jessie Seymour Irvine (1836-1887).

The music is played on an organ, and the congregation (the people in the church) sing the words.

J. S. Irvine

Moderato

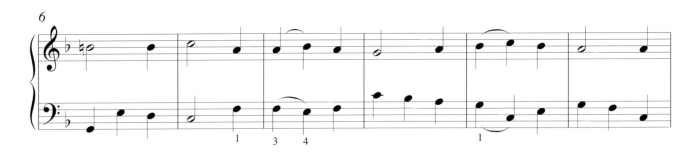

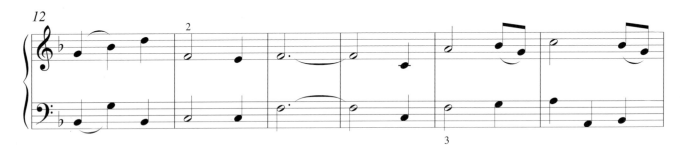

42

Jerusalem

This music was written to go with a poem called *Jerusalem*, by the English poet William Blake (shown right).

Charles Parry (1848-1918) was a great admirer of J. S. Bach. He studied and wrote about Bach's music and about the history of musical style.

Parry

Go down Moses

This is a type of song known as a spiritual (see page 37). Spirituals were first sung by slaves in America in the 18th and 19th centuries.

Many spirituals are based on stories from the bible. This one is about slaves in Ancient Egypt, who were led by a man called Moses.

44

Swing low, sweet chariot

This is another spiritual that was first sung by slaves. Sometimes they sang songs like this while they worked.

It is hard to know when it was composed, as people learned spirituals by heart and passed them on, instead of writing them down.

Descriptive music

All the pieces in this section of the book describe a scene or tell a story. But they are different from the theatre music that begins on page 6, because they were not written to accompany plays, songs and dances. There are no spoken words or actions either. You have to imagine the story or picture yourself while you listen to the music.

To help you to do this, some pieces have titles that tell you what the music is about. Others also have words written above the music to tell the players what is happening. During the 19th century, when descriptive music was very popular, the audience was sometimes given a booklet to read which explained the story. This meant they could follow what was happening while they listened to the music.

Scheherazade (see below)

A 19th century audience

Landscapes and scenery

Some music describes a place or landscape. Mendelssohn composed a piece of music called *The Hebrides Overture* (sometimes known as *Fingal's Cave*).

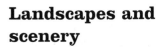

Fingal's cave, in the Hebrides

It was written in 1830 after he visited the Hebrides, a group of islands off the west coast of Scotland. He thought the scenery was so beautiful that he wrote a piece of music about it.

Many pieces were written to describe the country or area where the composer lived. Between 1872 and 1879, the Czech composer Smetana wrote a set of six pieces which he called *Ma Vlast* ("My Country"). Each one is about a different aspect of Czech countryside and culture. He called them "musical poems", because he thought they were so descriptive that the audience would feel as if they were reading poetry. Pieces like this are examples of a trend in music known as Nationalism (see page 23).

The River Moldau in Prague

Music that tells a story

Many composers have written music based on stories. For example, the Russian composer Rimsky-Korsakov based one of his pieces on *The Arabian Nights*, a large collection of folk tales. The music is called *Scheherazade*, after the woman who first told the stories.

Scheherazade telling her stories

Each movement has a title to tell the listeners which part of the story it represents. The first movement is called "The young prince and the young princess".

This type of music often uses special themes (melodies) for the main characters in the story. This helps listeners to recognize the people in the story when their themes are played. Sometimes it is also possible to tell the mood of the character. For example, if the theme is played very loudly, with drums in the background, it could mean that the character is angry.

Another Russian composer, Tchaikovsky, wrote a piece about the war between Russia and France in 1812. He used parts of the Russian national anthem to describe the triumphant feeling of the Russians as they finally beat the French. The music even includes cannons to create the sounds and atmosphere of a war. The piece is called the *1812 Overture*.

Russian soldiers fighting the French in 1812

Seasonal music

Sometimes music is written to describe different times of the day or year. Vivaldi wrote a set of pieces called *The Four Seasons*. It describes the way the seasons change throughout the year.

A scene from The Four Seasons

He wrote lots of comments above the music to say what was happening, such as "the dog barks" and "shivering with cold".

Haydn also gave descriptive titles to a lot of his music. He wrote three pieces to describe different parts of the day. These are called *le matin* ("Morning"), *le midi* ("Noon") and *le soir* ("Evening"). There are no words written above the music, but you can hear the mood change in each piece. *Le matin* has a slow introduction, as if the sun is rising. Then the music livens up as the day begins.

Music about feelings

Many composers have written music that describes their feelings and emotions. The French composer Berlioz fell in love with the actress Harriet Smithson after seeing her in a play. He was unable to arrange to meet her, so to attract her attention he wrote the *Symphonie fantastique* ("Fantastic symphony") about his feelings for her.

The story behind the piece is a mixture of facts, emotions, dreams and nightmares. At the first performance, the audience was given a printed copy of the story to read. The music expresses his feelings and is often very dramatic. Though Harriet Smithson was not at the concert, she and Berlioz later met, and were eventually married.

Harriet Smithson

Chopin composed many pieces called Nocturnes. They were written specially to create a mood or atmosphere, rather than to describe a specific place or event. Chopin used to play them for his friends in the evenings as a form of relaxation.

Chopin playing Nocturnes

Autumn

This tune by Antonio Vivaldi (1678-1741) is from *The Four Seasons*, a set of four violin concertos. Vivaldi learned the violin as a child.

His father was a violinist in the orchestra at St. Mark's Cathedral in Venice. Sometimes Vivaldi played there instead of his father.

Vivaldi

Vivaldi was born in Venice and lived there for most of his life. On the right you can see a picture of Venice during a carnival.

Carnivals and festivals were very common in Venice at this time. They were held in the city for almost six months of each year.

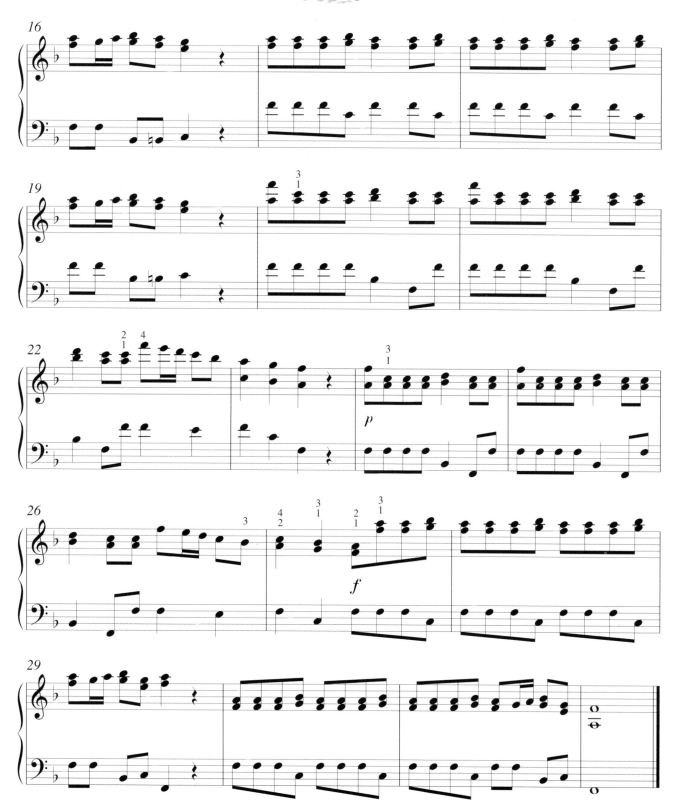

Nocturne

Felix Mendelssohn (1809-1847) first wrote this Nocturne as part of a descriptive overture called *A Midsummer Night's Dream*.

This piece was inspired by William Shakespeare's play (see below). Later he used the same tunes to write a longer piece to go with the play.

Mendelssohn

The story of *A Midsummer Night's Dream*

In Athens, Theseus is about to be married. Four lovers are in a wood nearby: Hermia and Lysander (who are in love), Demetrius (who loves Hermia) and Helena (who loves Demetrius). There are also six craftsmen rehearsing a play. Oberon, a fairy king, uses a magic love potion on his queen, Titania, and on Demetrius (to make him love Helena). In the confusion that follows, Titania falls in love with one of the craftsmen, who has been given a donkey's head by one of the fairies. The play ends with a triple wedding, the craftsmen's play and a fairy dance.

Oberon and his magical servant, Puck

50

When Mendelssohn first came across Shakespeare's play, he immediately decided to write a piece of music about it.

He was so excited about the music that he wrote to his sister, Fanny to tell her about it. Fanny (shown left) was also a talented composer.

Puck casts a spell on Bottom, giving him a donkey's head

A scene from the craftsmen's play

The triple wedding scene at the end of the play

Hebrides overture (Fingal's cave)

Mendelssohn was very popular in Britain, and he visited England ten times. You can find out more about this piece on page 46.

Mendelssohn loved the excitement of London. He spent much time going to concerts, operas and balls, and walking in Hyde Park.

Mendelssohn

Nocturne op.15, no.2

Fryderyk Chopin (1810-1849) was a Polish composer. He was also a brilliant pianist and teacher, and was famous for his delicate playing.

In fact, he did not give many public performances. But he often played for small groups of friends and admirers, even as a young boy.

Chopin

The piano shown on the right was given to Chopin during a visit to London in 1848. Unlike most other composers, Chopin did not write music for many different instruments. Almost everything he wrote was for the piano. The only music that he wrote for orchestra was to accompany large piano works. He composed a lot of his music while he was playing (called improvising), then wrote it down later.

Romeo and Juliet

This piece was written in 1869. It is called a fantasy overture because the audience has to imagine the story as they hear the music.

Each theme (or tune) represents a particular character from the story. This helps the listeners to know what is happening.

Tchaikovsky

Andante con moto

Tchaikovsky went to America in 1891. He found the people very friendly, and felt he was welcome there.

He was particularly impressed with the Capitol building, which he visited in Washington, D.C.

Promenade

This tune by Modest Musorgsky (1839-1881) represents the composer walking though an art gallery looking at paintings.

It is from a piece called *Pictures at an Exhibition*. The pictures he is looking at were painted by a close friend of his, Victor Hartmann.

Musorgsky

Vltava

Bedrich Smetana (1824-1884) was born in Bohemia (now the Czech Republic). He was very fond of his country and often wrote music about it.

This piece is from a larger work called *Ma Vlast* ("My Country"). *Vltava* is about the river Moldau which flows through Prague.

Smetana

Scheherazade

Nikolay Rimsky-Korsakov (1844-1908) wrote a lot of music based on fairy tales. This piece is based on a story called *The Arabian Nights*.

In the story, an evil sultan vows to marry and kill a different woman each day. Scheherazade saves herself by telling him stories.

Rimsky-Korsakov

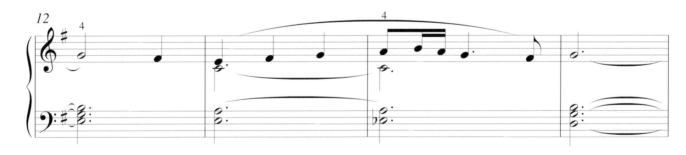

Each night, Scheherazade ends her story on a note of suspense. The sultan wants to know what happens next, so he cannot kill her.

After one thousand and one nights he decides she should be allowed to live. This tune is thought to represent a princess in one of the stories.

The girl with the flaxen hair

Claude Debussy (1862-1918) was a French composer. On the right you can see the town where he was born, called St. Germain-en-Laye.

He studied the piano at the Paris Conservatoire (a special school for music). But soon he became much more interested in composing.

Debussy

While he was a student, his teacher found him summer jobs working as a musician for wealthy patrons.

His first job was as a resident musician to a millionaire music-lover at her home, the Château de Chenonceaux (shown on the left).

Playing the pieces

On these pages you will find some hints on playing the pieces in this book. When you are learning a piece, it is often better to practise each hand separately, slowly at first, until you can play them both comfortably. Then try them at the correct speed, and lastly try playing with both hands together.

There are suggestions for fingerings in the music, but if these do not feel comfortable you could try to work out your own. If you want to begin with the simplest pieces in the book, try the Sleeping Beauty waltz on page 21 and the Eugene Onegin waltz on page 33.

Terzettino

Take care in bars 9, 22 and 28 with the semiquaver passages in thirds. Practise these bars on their own first. You may find bar 13 a little difficult. Try each hand separately until you are confident about the fingering, then play both hands together. In bars 26 and 27, play the left hand part very quietly so that you can still hear the chord above.

Fidelio

From the second beat in bar 5 to the first in bar 9, you need to play the left hand a little louder than the right.

The Barber of Seville overture

Play this piece lightly. The left-hand chords should be quieter than the right-hand notes.

Drinking song

You might want to practise the first few bars several times before trying the whole piece, to get the rhythm right. Make sure the left hand is very even and don't play the second and third beats louder than the first.

Anvil chorus

Make sure your hands keep absolutely together where they are playing the same rhythm (from bar 11 to 15).

Soldiers' chorus

Take care with the coda in bars 18 and 19. Make sure you play the thirds in the right hand at the correct speed.

March of the kings

The notes must be kept as short as possible especially in the left hand. Where two notes are slurred and the second has a dot over it, the second note should be very short.

Du und du

Keep the left hand very even and make sure the three-note chords are not too heavy.

Morning

Play this very smoothly and gently. There are lots of accidentals in the middle section of the piece (bars 8 to 16). Practise this section on its own first to make sure you are confident of the notes.

Flower duet

When both hands play quavers together, make sure the notes are even. Take care not to speed up during the longer quaver passages (such as bars 5 to 7). Practise bars 26 to 30 on their own until you can play them smoothly.

Pizzicati

This piece should be played very lightly, with each note as short as possible. Try it slowly at first and then speed it up.

Sleeping Beauty waltz

Emphasize the first beat of each bar in the left hand, but keep it smooth.

Musette

Practise the right hand part of bars 13 to 18 on its own at first. Once you are familiar with the accidentals and the rhythm, then add the left hand. Try to make a difference between the slurred and the staccato notes.

German dance

Make sure you count carefully when both hands are resting, and keep the tempo even.

Minuet in A

Practise both hands separately until there are no mistakes. Then put the parts together very slowly and gradually speed up. You do not need to play too quickly, but you must keep a steady pace, especially the left hand.

The Blue Danube waltz no.1

From bar 26 to the end, in the left hand, try to make the second and third beats of the bar slightly quieter than the first.

Hungarian dance no.5

Practise the right hand of bars 13 to 15 on its own. When you can play it at the correct speed, add the left hand.

Dance of the hours

The second note in each pair of quavers should be as short as possible.

Slavonic dance

Practise the rhythm in the first two bars, as this appears throughout the piece.

Eugene Onegin waltz

Make sure you hold the dotted minim right to the end of each bar.

Norwegian dance

Play this piece very lightly. Practise it slowly until you can play all the notes accurately.

Polovtsian dance

The rhythm is fairly difficult so try playing it very slowly at first. The left hand helps to keep the rhythm, so add this as soon as you can.

Wachet auf!

You may need to play this slowly until you get used to the fingering.

Jesu, joy of man's desiring

It is easier to count this as three beats in a bar. Keep a steady pace without playing it too slowly, to make it flow.

The Heavens are telling the glory of God

The left hand is fairly tricky, especially in bars 6 to 8. Practise these bars until you can play them without any mistakes before you put the two parts together.

The Lord's my shepherd

Take care not to rush this piece. Play it fairly slowly, keeping the notes even.

Jerusalem

Maestoso means "majestically". Play it very boldly and at a steady pace.

Go down Moses

Practise the rhythm in bar 3, it appears several times in the piece. Bars 12 and 13 may need some extra practice.

Swing low, sweet chariot

The rhythm in the right hand is fairly difficult. Make sure you can play it confidently before you add the left hand.

Autumn

The right hand has thirds almost all the way through the piece. You need to practise these until you can play them evenly. The left hand has the same rhythm, so make sure you play the two parts absolutely together.

Nocturne

This should be very gentle. Make sure the accompaniment is always very soft to allow the tune to come through.

Hebrides overture (Fingal's cave)

From bar 9 to the end the left hand part is fairly difficult. Learn the left hand on its own before putting the two parts together.

Nocturne op.15, no.2

Bar 7 has a very tricky rhythm in the right hand. You need to practise this bar slowly and accurately before playing the whole piece.

Romeo and Juliet

Make sure you keep the left hand very even. Play the left hand a little quieter than the right hand to stop it from sounding too heavy.

Promenade

The time signature changes every bar. Try to keep a steady crotchet beat, placing a little more emphasis on the first beat of each bar.

Vltava

Try to play this very smoothly, without leaving any gaps between the notes.

Scheherazade

Hold the chords in the left hand for the full length of the notes. Keep the right hand flowing smoothly.

The girl with the flaxen hair

Take care with the rhythm in bars 14 to 15 and 33 to 34. The fingering is fairly hard, so you will need to practise it until it feels comfortable.

Index

First published in 1994 by Usborne Publishing Ltd, 83-85 Saffron Hill, London EC1N 8RT, England. Copyright © 1994 Usborne Publishing Ltd.

The name Usborne and the device are Trade Marks of Usborne Publishing Ltd. All